Mobile Marketing Mania

Trey Patrick

Copyright © 2012 Trey Patrick
All rights reserved.
ISBN: 1479356603
ISBN-13: 978-147935607

CONTENTS

What Exactly is 'Mobile Marketing', How Does It Work and Why Should I Care As a Business Owner?	5
The Real Reason For Getting Excited About Mobile Marketing	12
What Is Mobile?	16
How Do I Actually Do Mobile Marketing In Practice?	35
Mobile Websites	50
Summary	61

What Exactly is 'Mobile Marketing', How Does it Work & Why Should I Care As a Business Owner?

If you're like most other business owners, you will have heard that you "must" do mobile marketing.

And most likely, no one has really sat down with you and explained to you

- **WHY** you should care, (or: *if* you should care),
- **WHAT** "Mobile Marketing" really is, and
- **HOW** it works in practice

And that's exactly the purpose of this short guide on "Mobile Marketing Mania":

After reading this guide you'll have a good enough understanding of this whole "Mobile Marketing thing", so you can make an informed decision on

- Whether you actually want to do Mobile Marketing,
- Whether you want to do it yourself, or rather get an Mobile Marketing service provider to do it for you, and
- If you're planning to outsource the work, how to select a reliable and trustworthy service provider

Question 1: Why Should You Care? (or Should You Care At All?)

Let's start by looking at the most important question: "WHY?", so you can decide whether you even want to keep reading!

If you think about it, there are 2 main ways you can increase your profits:

You can either

- **increase turnover, or**
- **decrease cost of sales/expenses**

So when we look at the "WHY" of doing anything on the Internet, it is with these 2 questions in mind: does Mobile Marketing (or any other Internet related activity) help increase turnover or decrease the cost of sales?

With that in mind, let's first look at the "obvious" reasons everyone keeps telling you about:

The Facts

The mobile revolution is pretty much global and it touches all customers. Over the last 5 years alone, 2 Billion new users have gone "mobile".

It is estimated that in 2012, around 149 Million new mobile *smartphones* will ship in the US alone.

In other words:

Mobile phones are everywhere, and people use them everywhere.

The table below gives you an overview over how people *use* their mobile phones in practice.

This data from a recent ComScore study (http://www.comscore.com/Press_Events/Press_Releases/2012/7/comScore_Reports_May_2012_U.S._Mobile_Subscriber_Market_Share and http://www.comscore.com/Press_Events/Press_Releases/2011/7/comScore_Reports_May_2011_U.S._Mobile_Subscriber_Market_Share) shows you how people used their mobile phones a year ago, and how the usage patterns have evolved over the last year.

It is obvious, that the most common way of how people use their mobile phones is for sending and receiving text-messages: the **average user receives around 40 text-messages a day**, and that trend is going up!

What's also interesting to observe is that the use of downloaded apps and the usage of the browser on a smartphone has gone up by 12.5 and 10 percentage points respectively over the last year.

As you can see in the "May-12" column, **three-quarters of all users responded that they're texting regularly**, and about 50% responded that they are using apps and the browser.

Meaning:

Your biggest potential to tap into the 'natural' user-behavior is by engaging your prospects and clients through

1. text messaging,
2. apps and
3. the browser

Now, the fact alone that people buy and own more mobile phones isn't very exciting in itself (unless you're selling mobile phones of course).

And the fact that they're texting, using apps and the browser doesn't necessarily help you either.

What is however exciting for you as a business owner is this:

> Mobile users tend to use their phones in a way that's very different from someone who is using a desktop computer: they use their mobile devices to make a *purchasing* decision!

The 'Real' Reason For Getting Excited About Mobile Marketing

According to internal Microsoft research, **mobile consumers tend to take immediate action** after doing their online (re)search, much more so than someone who is using a desktop computer.

In practice, the purchasing decision is done and the *transaction completed within minutes or hours*, when mobile, compared to days, or sometimes weeks when using a PC.

What's even more exciting is that **most of those searches are local** in nature (in other words: people are looking for a solution locally), and they are nearly twice as likely to take action as someone using a PC.

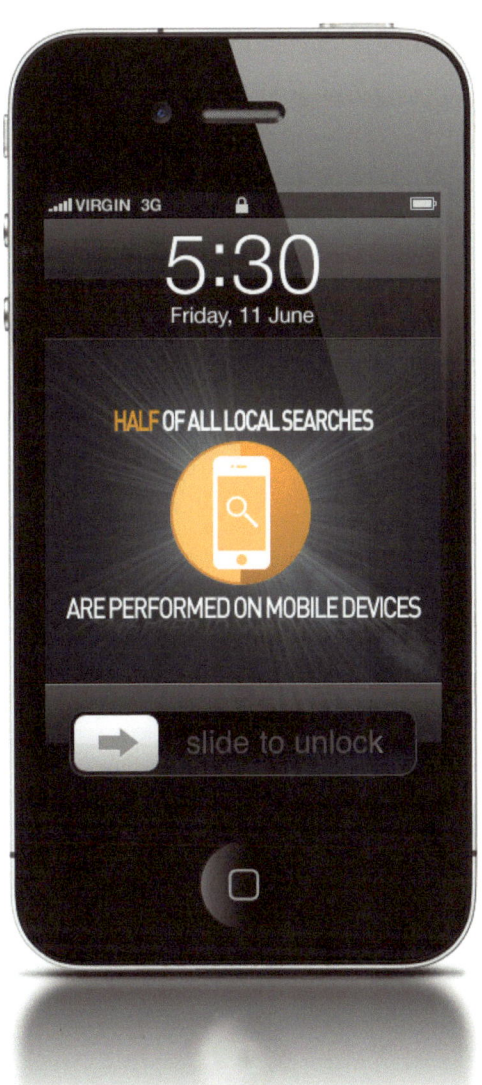

When someone uses their mobile device to do a local search, they are very close to making a purchasing decision, and they can **easily be influenced by a coupon, a special offer, and of course the convenient location.**

In practice, it has been observed that mobile phone users have a stronger desire *for **instant gratification*** than someone doing a search on a PC: if they cannot find an item in one store, often they will use their mobile phone to search for a nearby store that has the item in stock – rather than ordering it online!

Meaning: the mindset of someone using a mobile phone to make a purchasing decision is not necessarily to find the best price, **but to get the desired item fast and in a convenient way.**

Another benefit of mobile marketing is that users have an **increased brand-recall compared to traditional advertising,** and – interestingly - the vast majority remember the specific call to action!

And as you've probably experienced yourself, this is unheard of with traditional advertising!

To sum up:

Consumers use their mobile devices to find answers to the questions,

"What do I need now?

What do I need in the next couple of hours?"

And then they go out and get it!

Question #2: 'What' Is Mobile?

Ok, this may sound a little silly, but there is far more to "mobile marketing" than just text-messaging.

So, in the following, we'll cover the most important aspects of mobile marketing.

And these are:

1. **text-messaging (also known as SMS) and multi-media messaging (MMS)**
2. **mobile apps**
3. **mobile websites**
4. **(mobile) coupons**
5. **Quick-response (QR) codes**

The first three are obviously the ones that are most commonly used by mobile phone users as you saw from the ComScore data above.

The coupons and QR codes are great ways of getting people to take action – but only if it's a good fit.

Let's look at these in turn:

SMS & MMS

SMS stands for "Short Message Service" and it's the way phones send and receive text messages. Often, SMS is also referred to as 'Text Messaging'.

SMS is text only, whereas MMS (Multimedia Message Service) can include audio, video, and pictures. In addition to the multimedia -content of the message, the MMS message can include up to 1,000 characters of text, quite a bit more than the 160 characters you get with an SMS.

For the time being, we'll cover primarily SMS, and come back to the uses of MMS later on.

What's interesting about these types of messages is that around **95% of them are opened and read within the first 60mins of receiving them.**

When you compare that with a typical open-rate of around **5% for emails**, you can start to see how a well-timed, targeted message can help you do very effective marketing.

There are many reasons why SMS have such a high open-rate, but ONE very important one is that the typical SPAM rate for SMS is below 10% (only one in 10 messages will be unsolicited), whereas for emails, well, just have a look at the spam-folder of your email-inbox.

Meaning: people *trust* the messages they get in their SMS inbox!

So, how can you use SMS to attract clients, increase turnover and decrease cost of sales?

You can use SMS-marketing in 2 main ways:

1. SMS-marketing on its own is "just" a direct marketing method or tool like many others (think email or direct marketing). Meaning, you can send out offers, and people (hopefully) take action on them and the end-result is a business transaction.

   However,

2. SMS-marketing can (and should) be used to *enhance* any other form of advertising and marketing you are doing!

   And it does this in 2 ways:

   2. It ties different mediums together very nicely: you can easily connect typical mass-advertising mediums (print, TV, radio) with your mobile website, your mobile apps or your social media presence through something called "short-

codes" (where your prospects send a short message to a given number, we'll cover this shortly)

2. It lets you build very detailed customer profiles (we'll cover how this is done later) meaning that when you send out a message, you know it's going to be on-target!

   Which of course increases the likelihood of your prospect taking action, and coming to your store and buying something.

When your customers opt-in to your mobile marketing program then you know that you have someone who is likely to buy from you.

And because you have their **permission** to send them text messages, **you can reach them anytime and anywhere with a 95% open rate.**

The same principle applies to MMS, and in the "how-to" section later on, you'll discover how best to use SMS & MMS in practice.

Mobile Apps

Although the use of mobile apps is going up quite dramatically as you saw from the ComScore data above, there are very few applications where a custom mobile app for a small business really makes sense.

Why?

There are several reasons, but the biggest one is the lack of visibility:

You can think of an app like a closed shop without any signs on the outside.

Unless someone is specifically looking for your app, they won't find your business.

A mobile website is typically visible in the search-engines, so if someone is looking for "Italian restaurant NYC", they'll find a list of Italian restaurants in NYC.

But they won't find a list of apps by the Italian restaurants in NYC.

True, if you have the resources, an existing "mobile" list and a solid social media presence where your business has a strong following, then you can successfully launch an app and get enough traction to make it worthwhile.

But, for most small businesses this is not a reality and they cannot justify the investment of time and resources for something that is pretty much a long-term strategy.

Then there is the fact that most apps are only opened a couple of times (those apps that get opened repeatedly are either really useful tools people use all the time, like the Facebook-app to access their FB-account, the weather-forecast, that kind of thing, or silly things like fun games to play whilst stuck in traffic)

The online retailer shoes.com did a simple test where they compared how much revenue they were generating via either a mobile website or a custom app.

The **mobile website generated 80% more revenue than the app.**

We hope we've sold you on the idea of <u>not</u> getting a mobile app as the first step into the "mobile marketing world".

Now, are all mobile apps bad?

No, there are a few examples where it makes sense to have a custom mobile app developed, and that is when you have a loyalty or reward program and/or a VIP club or if you have a large ecommerce side to your business.

One such example is the Starbucks app, which lets you track your reward-stars and also acts as a payment method.

As you can see, as we mentioned above: it's an app that gets used on a very regular basis, and is hence a 'useful' app.

Apps can also use more the inbuilt features of your phone. So if it makes sense to use the "location" functionality, the in-built camera to scan codes, and to offer coupons and easy checkout methods, then sure, an app might be the way forward.

But for most small businesses we recommend getting their "mobile feet" wet with a mobile site first.

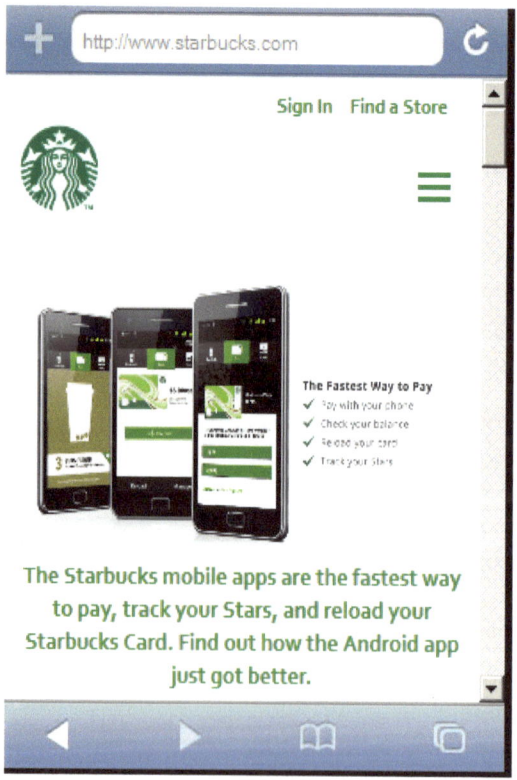

Summary

Mobile apps are generally **not recommended as a first step** into the mobile marketing world, you are much better off investing your marketing budget in a mobile website, where

- You can get the same level (or better) of interaction with your prospects and customers,

- Plus you can use a mobile website to build your SMS-list, and of course

- You get found in the search-engines, whereas an app isn't.

Mobile Websites

A mobile website is a website like any other website, the only difference is that it is optimized for the small screen-size, and the fact that navigating around a website, and entering data is cumbersome to say the least on the small screen of a smartphone.

In the following image, you first see the Starbucks.com website, the way you would view it on a desktop computer.

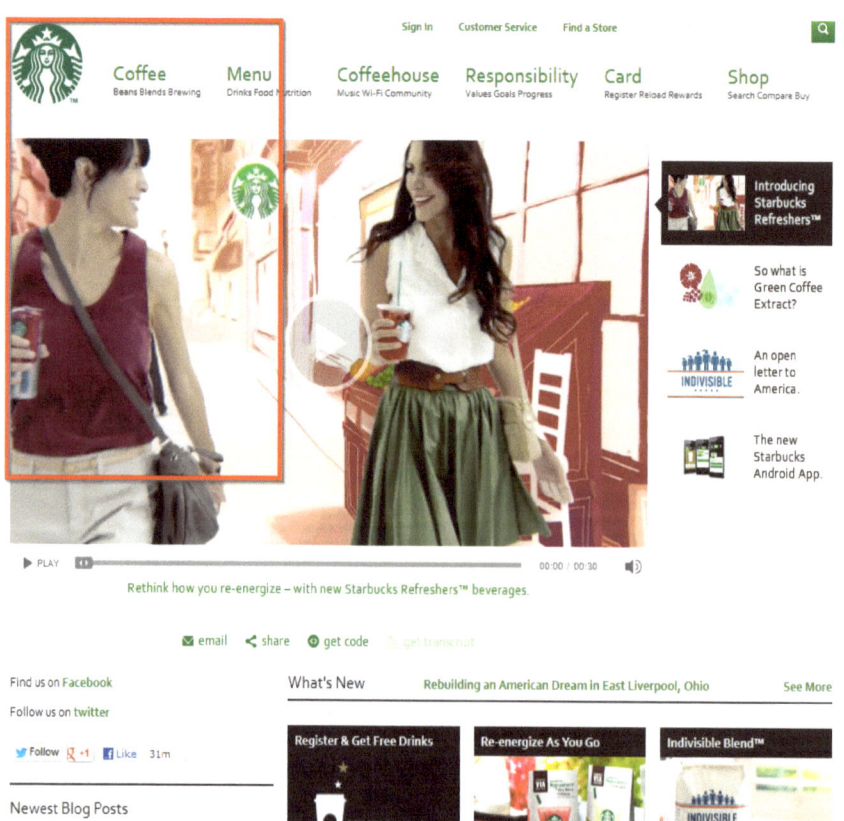

The small red frame illustrates what you would see if Starbucks did not have a mobile website: only a very small proportion of the overall information available on the screen.

This would create a rather dissatisfying user-experience on a smartphone, which is why most big companies have a mobile version of their website.

The next image shows the mobile version of the Starbucks.com website:

As you can see, there are only two items in the menu at the top (1): "Sign in" and "Find a store" (these are the most important things people on the move are doing: it's back to instant gratification, "where can I find the nearest store?")

The rest of the menu is hidden in the small box with the 3 horizontal bars (2): when you click on there, the menu opens and the user can select from the different options.

25

The video from the desktop version above has been replaced by an image (3) to make sure the site loads faster.

Finally, in order to avoid vertical scrolling (there is no horizontal scrolling to begin with), there are 3 additional pages immediately accessible by clicking on the small grey dots below the main image (4).

This way the user has access to a lot of content without having to scroll at all.

And at the same time, the home-page (and any other page) is kept clean and smart-looking, and the user always knows where they are and where they want to get to.

Here are some more examples of mobile sites:

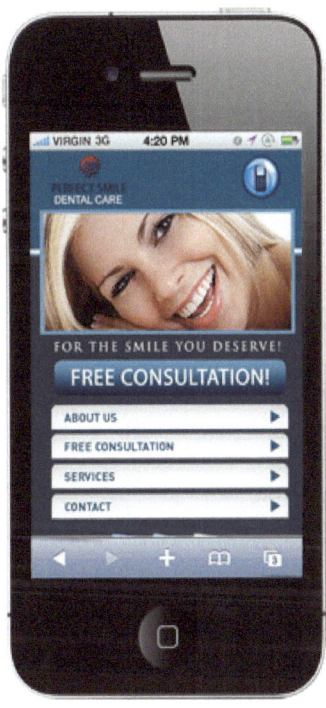

Coupons

Alright, let's start with a little reality check:

If you've been around for a little while, you may have tried coupons in print-advertising (newspaper?)

Actually, statistically speaking, you probably haven't, because you have heard over and over again **that coupons don't work.**

And it's true:

When you have coupons in a newspaper, then <u>unless</u> you have a system in place that tracks how they perform, and you've trained your staff to keep entering all returned coupons in the system, and you have an offer that converts really well (aka: people love it;-), then coupons can be pretty tricky to make profitable.

Fortunately for you, this is where "mobile marketing" really shines!

See, you don't have to invest in some expensive newspaper ad just to find out whether or not a coupon works.

First of all, with online technology, you can easily do something that's called "split-testing":

What you are doing is sending one coupon to a one (small) segment of your list, and another coupon to another (small) segment of your list.

Then you simply observe, which one works better, and you then send the winner to all those who haven't seen the coupon yet.

Or of course, you keep refining your coupon to get even better conversions.

Btw, you are of course not limited to creating one 'best' coupon offer.

With online technology, you can easily create highly converting coupons targeted at different types of customers.

That way you very quickly hone in on offers that get your prospects and customers excited, meaning more visitors to your business!

Secondly, mobile coupons are highly measurable – you can accurately measure which coupons were redeemed, who redeemed them, when they redeemed them, what else they bought etc.

With paper coupons, this requires quite a bit of additional 'logging & tracking' work, but here, because everything is virtual already, you have all the numbers you need at your fingertips.

QR Codes

QR codes are the barcodes of the online world.

The only difference is that instead of using a bunch of parallel lines like the barcodes do, the QR codes are 2-dimensional as you can see in the example on the right.

QR stands for "quick response": the idea behind this is that you do not need to enter a lengthy URL or a website, but instead scan the QR code with the phone-camera, which then redirects you to the target URL.

In practice, you can use QR codes to forward the user to pretty much any online destination.

This could be

- a website
- YouTube Video
- Google Maps Location
- Twitter
- Facebook
- LinkedIn
- FourSquare
- App Store Download

- iTunes Link
- Plain Text
- Telephone Number
- Skype Call
- SMS Message
- Email Address
- Email Message
- Contact Details (VCARD)
- Event (VCALENDAR)
- Wifi Login (Android Only)
- Paypal Buy Now Link
- A coupon

For this to work, the user has to install a QR-reader app on their smartphone. (Which btw these readers are free and coming basic on ALL new smartphones…)

This app then decides what the right application is to view the information (email, browser, text-viewer, …) and opens that application with the corresponding information the QR code is "pointing to".

(Go Ahead... scan it... It goes to my main website)

The QR codes have a little bit of redundancy built in, meaning that if a few of the little black and white dots aren't 'perfect', the QR code can still work.

Some people are exploiting this in a very creative way: you can e.g. put your company logo into a QR code, and the code will still work.

On the right, you see an example of a QR code that has the BBC logo embedded.

One problem with QR codes is that there are ways for spammers and hackers to distribute malware through QR codes.

The more of this kind of information is reported in the media, the less likely people are to use QR codes.

But, if you decide to use QR codes in your marketing, you should make sure to use managed QR codes where you can get analytics of how often a particular code is being scanned, plus by redirecting the visitor to different destinations, you can once again do easy split-testing to find out what offers work for a particular target audience.

Question #3: How Do I Actually Do Mobile Marketing In Practice?

In this section, you'll find plenty of tips on how to implement the various mobile tools.

SMS/MMS

Remember, SMS helps with your marketing in 2 ways: you can use it to

1. do direct marketing campaigns to reach individuals with very targeted messages

2. enhance other forms of advertising you are doing

How can you do the 'direct marketing' part?

In a nutshell, here is what you do:

- You build a 'list' of people who are interested in receiving SMS messages from you
- You can then send targeted messages to that list

In that sense, it is very similar to having a list of email addresses, or even doing a direct mail campaign, where you rent a list of names, and send them a direct mail piece.

But, as explained earlier, there are **huge differences** in how effective these mediums are:

Because there is that inherent trust, resulting in that high open-rate, combined with the ability to do very targeted message-campaigns, SMS-based marketing has a huge advantage over the other forms of mass-marketing mentioned.

To give you a few examples:

I have a coffee shop in town that we started a SMS text marketing campaign... In less than 6 months, we have 1179 people on their list who has stood up and said...

"Please text me any specials or offers you have because I will take you up on it..."

Imagine you're a restaurant owner, and you have overstocked on a certain item. It is now very easy to create an SMS campaign, offering a special deal on that item for anyone who shows up this afternoon.

The same goes for any business that has to deal with 'slow times': whenever there aren't enough customers, you simply send out an SMS and make your customers an irresistible offer.

However, and this is a **very important point many people who get into SMS-marketing overlook:**

SMS **is best used to deliver time-sensitive promotions that are designed to move the hottest items at the highest price points** instead of using it to just ditch overstocked items.

Remember the "instant gratification" we mentioned earlier?

The key here is time-sensitive, often combined with exclusivity that makes the big difference - and we'll cover more of this later on.

Another example: say you're a real-estate agent: nothing easier than sending out an update to anyone who has expressed interest in a particular property, or is looking for just the type of property that has just come onto the market.

Another way you can use text-messaging is for appointment-reminders – this has been shown to reduce the no-show rate significantly, meaning you don't find yourself with nothing to do, just because a client didn't show up.

How Do I build a list or prospects in practice?

The technical part of this is relatively straightforward:

Either people just give you their cell-number, or you use something called **"short-codes" and "keywords":**

The short-code is a 5 or 6 digit phone-number which is allocated to you by the carriers, and your prospects then send a short keyword to that short phone-number.

These short-codes are approved individually by the carriers, which is one of the reasons why the overall spam-volume is so extremely low: if you don't play ball and get too many complaints, then the carrier simply terminates your short-code, and you can no longer send text-messages.

In other words: you are only leasing the short-code, you don't own it!

In practice, most businesses don't have a unique short-code, but share it with several other businesses, meaning it is much cheaper than having your own dedicated short-code.

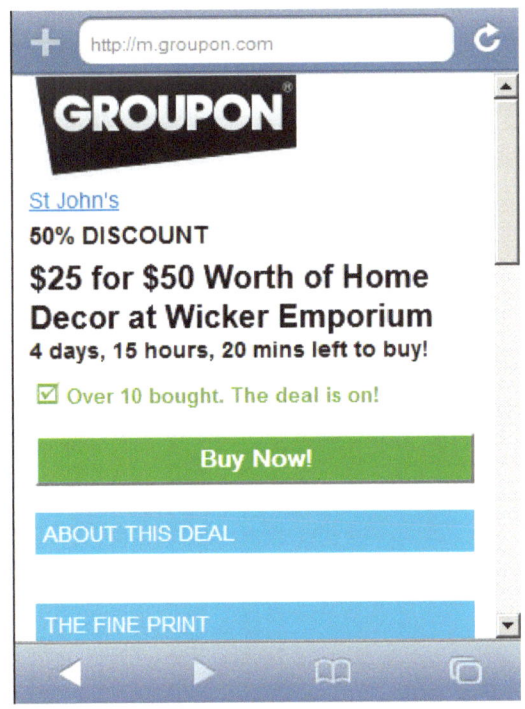

What is unique on the other hand is of course **the *keyword***, which is the short text the user sends to your short-code.

So, as an example, you could have the keyword "VIPCLUB" and the short-code 123456 and whenever someone sends a text-message with the text "VIPCLUB" to the number 123456, you can do all kinds of things with that information, including of course storing the number of the phone from which the text was sent.

Incidentally, people do not necessarily need to send a message from their phone to be added to your list, they can also submit their request via a web-interface.

The beauty of this system is that you don't need a smartphone to be able to use short-codes!

Meaning: while the use of smartphones certainly is going up dramatically, for the time being there are still a very substantial number of phones that do not have smart-phone capability (and hence cannot use things like QR-code readers, go to a website etc).

And that's about it – from the technical perspective.

In practice – although not difficult – there are a few specific steps you need to take to make sure your signup-process is 100% compliant (so you don't get kicked out by the carrier), but that is beyond the scope of this whitepaper.

If you would like us to explain to you what you need to look out for when creating your signup process, feel free to contact us for a free consultation at (706) 389-4796.

Or visit us on the web at GeorgiaMobileMarketing.com

The second part of the signup equation is this:

How do you get people to actually sign up to your list?

You may be familiar with the classic "squeeze" page on the Internet, where someone offers you a free report, or a video or similar in exchange for your email address.

The same principle applies here:

You offer something of value, and in exchange the user gives you their contact details and their permission to contact them through SMS marketing.

Now, because of the nature of mobile, the classic "here is a big report" approach does work, but it is not necessarily the best way of getting users involved.

Methods that are much better suited to "mobile" (and which are better integrated with your overall marketing strategy) are

- Polls & surveys
- Contests & sweepstakes
- VIP-club membership & loyalty/rewards program

Polls & surveys, and contests & sweepstakes tap into the viral nature of the SMS-medium, and VIP-club memberships let you do what we referred to earlier:

Sell hot products at a premium, rather than discounting everything and only getting people into your story via "money off" coupons.

Take e.g. a popular restaurant with long waiting lists.

If there is a cancellation, you can now send a quick message to your VIP list and tell them about the table that has become available.

Normally, they'd have to wait (probably for a long time) to get a table without a reservation, here's their chance to jump to the front of the line, just because they're in your VIP club.

In general, the more you treat your VIP list like true VIPs, instead of a "let's get rid off some overstock" outlet, the more success you'll have with it.

There are plenty of ways to get traffic to your mobile offers:

You can (and should) include your short-codes with any traditional form of advertising you are doing (newspaper ads, TV, radio, ...), you can do online-advertising (there is even mobile-phone specific advertising), you can use your social media presence, incentivize referrals, the list goes on.

Ok, great, so you can build a list of prospects, now you might be wondering:

"Excellent, I can now send messages to my list every day, or can I?"

No, (un)fortunately not!

Remember the trust-thing we discussed earlier?

If you start sending out daily emails, you'll quickly get labeled a "spammer" and people will unsubscribe from your list very quickly.

Having said that, one of the great advantages of SMS-marketing is that you can *market to your prospects 100% legally*!

When done properly, there is nothing spammy about SMS-marketing (hence the high trust-factor) – quite the contrary, people look forward to your messages.

The beauty of the system is: you are required to tell anyone who signs up how many messages they will be getting at most – so there's never a surprise, and you can easily test what rate of messages gives you the highest signup rate.

To sum up:

SMS-marketing is great for reducing advertising costs, because of 3 factors:

1. Due to the high "trust" factor, open-rates are high and you get great responses to your marketing

2. You can tailor your offers much better than say with email, print-advertising, direct mail etc, because in the process of building your list, you can collect very detailed information about the likes, needs and desires of your target audience, so you know what the market wants to hear from you

3. SMS-marketing enhances any other form of marketing you are doing

How Do You 'Enhance' Other Forms Of Advertising?

One thing we haven't mentioned before is that you can use SMS marketing in 2 very different ways, which goes back to your strategic objectives:

You can either use it to let people request some information (text for info) or you can use it to get people to join your list (text to join).

Text For Info

Text For Info implies that there is no signup required.

This is a great first step to get people to check out what you've got to offer without them having to 'hand over' their contact details.

It's a little bit like the "I'm just browsing" visitor to your business.

Until they're satisfied that they're likely to find what they are looking for, they are not overly keen to talk to a sales-assistant.

Examples could be information on a property, like the schools in the proximity, local transport and so on for a real-estate listing.

It's just good, solid information, but no need to go any further.

Only once the user is satisfied that this might be a good deal, then they can and will move forward and give you their contact details.

The Text For Info aspect is hence great to start conversations with prospects, enhance your traditional advertising like print-ads, radio & TV advertising, cinema advertising and so on.

You can also use it to attract fans to your social media presence, ask for feedback, arrange a call-back and many other options of creating that first point of contact.

The beauty of this is at the same time as you're offering your prospects good, solid information, you are also tracking the performance of your individual offline ads.

You simply use different keywords for your print and your radio ads, and you'll quickly see which one generates the better response, so you can focus more of your marketing budget on the medium that works best for you.

Note, in sufficiently large towns and cities, your newspaper should be able to run different ads for different regions where the newspaper is published. Make sure to use different keywords in the different regions so you can measure where you are getting the best response (and no, the newspaper sales-reps are not going to like this, because obviously you are not going to buy advertising in areas that generate no response)

Text To Join

The obvious reason for using a Text To Join approach is to get prospects onto your list, so you can keep marketing to them and make more repeat-sales.

The not-so-obvious reason is that once they are on your list, you can start building customer profiles, and then send specific targeted offers to the appropriate segments of your list.

Over time you are building up a better and better picture of what your customers want, so you only send them offers they are likely to respond to.

There are obviously many different ways you can do this. So, if you would like to arrange for a complimentary strategy session where we help you figure out what approach might fit your business best, feel free to contact us at (706) 389-4796.

MMS

MMS supports a wide range of media, including video, audio, pictures, slide-shows etc.

That means you probably already have quite a bit of useful content you can use for MMS-campaigns and if not – it can be created relatively easily and quickly.

Now, because of the multi-media aspect of MMS, one of the main applications of using MMS is to do the "soft" part of your marketing - evoke feelings to create brand awareness and brand loyalty.

Basically, you tell a story people can connect with.

And one of the best ways for doing this is to capture behind the scenes content that's not shared anywhere else (remember the whole VIP-thing?). See, because it's exclusive, users start looking forward to your messages – and isn't that something we all want: customer who are looking forward to our marketing?

Other ways of using multi-media content is when you have "virtual" content to show to your prospects, but you cannot be physically present at all times.

An example would be a real-estate agent who puts all the relevant information about a property into an MMS (images, video, contact info, written description) which a passer-by can request when they see the 'for-sale' sign outside a property.

But, as you know by now, the same effect can be achieved with a well-designed mobile website.

And of course: MMS don't work on traditional mobile phones, only on smartphones.

So, for the time being, our recommendation is:

Get the hang of using SMS properly to connect and enhance the various part or your marketing, then, once you have identified a particular group of prospects and/or customers who mostly use smartphones AND they would likely respond to "behind the scenes" type content (because e.g. they are part of your VIP club), then start adding MMS to your marketing mix.

Mobile Websites

The 'Technical bit'

Most businesses have a 'normal' website these days. And quite a few of those websites run on a content management system like Wordpress, Joomla or TYPO3.

There are so-called plugins (little bits of code you install on your website) that automatically convert your normal website into a mobile website.

And although some of the results are actually visually acceptable to the user, there is a major drawback of this approach:

Google and the other search-engines cannot tell that it is a mobile site.

And that is a problem and here is why:

Currently and in the foreseeable future, **the search-engines regard normal websites and mobile websites as 2 separate entities.**

The reason for this should by now be obvious:

The search-behavior of someone online is <u>very different</u> from someone who is searching for something on their mobile device.

So the search-engines 'know' this and they try to serve up content that is most suited to the particular modality.

Now, if your site is a normal site and it is just using a plugin to 'fake' a mobile site, then the search-engines 'think' that it is a normal site, and they will treat it as such: namely preferably show it for 'normal' searches, not for mobile searches.

What to do in practice

So, in practice what you should do is set up a so-called sub-domain (typically, the "www" at the beginning of your domain name is replaced by "m") and install a mobile specific site on there.

So, if your normal site is

http://www.yoursite.com

then your mobile site would live on

http://m.yoursite.com

and your normal site then redirects to your mobile site ("redirect" means that if the site recognizes that it's being viewed by a mobile device, it'll automatically serve up the "m." site.

You may have heard about .mobi domains – these are not essential to have, but if you already have yours, or you'd like to reserve it to protect your brand, all you'd then do is redirect the .mobi to the "m." domain.

**** I personally like to use a .mobi with entire different hosting for my clients because it is quickly being noticed that this gives you ANOTHER website in the search engines AND mobile sites are starting to rank for keywords just like another website.

This is ANOTHER reason I don't use the easy to make templates you find on the web that will transform your site into a mobile site in minutes. All this site is doing is shrinking your website and not creating an entire new website.

The way my team develops mobile websites take longer but in the end you're looking at an entire complete website.

The 'Design' Bit

When designing a mobile website, you have to think again how and why people are using their mobile devices:

- **They are unlikely to enter any significant amount of information** (they mini-keyboards are just too cumbersome) and

- **They are after instant gratification** (the attention span of a mobile searcher is even shorter than that of someone who is on a PC)

These things mean:

Streamline your site as much as you can!

It has to be easier and faster to navigate.

That means:

1. fewer (and smaller) graphics,

2. fewer (or none) and shorter videos,

3. fewer menu-items for navigation

4. use click-to-call functionality whenever possible, so your visitors don't have to type in your phone-number

5. reduce the number of links on the page

6. avoid using forms and tables – hardly anyone is going to type in big messages anyway

7integrate a map if possible – make your site as visual as possible. Remember: you can't print out directions, but with a good map it's relatively easy to find your business.

Here are a couple of examples of what a good, clean mobile website can look like:

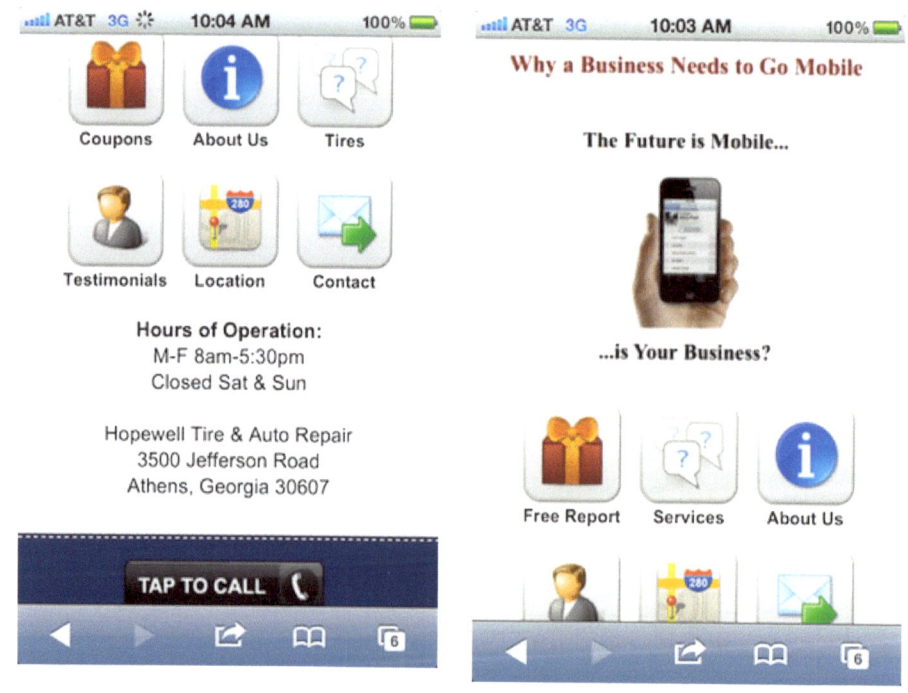

Coupons

With coupons, it is essential that you start with clearly defined objectives to make them work.

Do you want to use coupons to reach an audience you wouldn't reach otherwise?

Is your main aim to increase the average order size?

Do you want to encourage referrals?

Are you aiming to increase the overall life-time value (LTV) or your customer?

All of these are good things to aim for, but depending on what your goal is, different types of offers will be required.

The good news is:

Although you can always 'guess' what a good offer might be, in reality you will have to test.

And yes, that's *good* news.

Because far too many business owners spend forever trying to figure out what the 'best' offer might be, do one campaign, see no results and never use coupons again.

See, there are so many factors that affect how a particular target audience will respond to your offer, that it is nearly impossible to make the right 'guess'.

So, rather than worry about making the right or wrong choice, just start with something that makes more or less sense, and test yourself to success.

And because it's so easy and cheap with mobile technology, you can do this very, very quickly and affordably – and certainly much cheaper and faster than putting a coupon in the newspaper.

Now, there's one big topic we need to cover, and that is

Redemption

How do your prospects or customers actually redeem a coupon?

Here are the most common ways:

- The customer presents the code on their mobile phone, and the cashier simply gives them a discount.

- The customer presents the code on their mobile phone, and the cashier enters it into the checkout system (much better, as all your tracking is done automatically now)

- Alternatively to entering the code manually, the cashier can scan it – if you have the technology. In this case the code is typically in the form of a barcode, meaning you can only view it on a smartphone. If you go down this route, you should make sure to have an email-to-print function, so those who do not have a smartphone can receive an email with the code and print it out on their desktop computer.

- The coupons are downloaded to a reward-program, and the customer can then use the 'credit' as they please. If you have a reward-program app, these can then e.g. display which of the coupons have been redeemed, and when they expire (if you have an expiration date, which is highly recommended)

Now, although this sounds straightforward, in practice you will have to train your staff – you will not believe the number of times the checkout staff are totally confused by the coupon they're seeing (often for the first time), then ask the customer to print it out ("from my mobile phone???"), and so on.

It is nothing complicated, but you and your staff should run through the whole process a few times to make sure you are creating a positive experience for your customer – you certainly don't want to lose them now as a repeat customer simply because of a bad checkout experience.

This is of course not an issue if the coupon is applied straight to the reward-program where the coupon/discount is applied automatically at the checkout.

QR Codes

You have probably seen QR codes in many places, like posters, bill-boards, t-shirts, business-card, menus, for-sale signs put up by real-estate agents and so on.

So, you might be thinking: "I must get a QR code and put it all over my marketing material"

Well, that depends.

See, QR codes are really only useful if your target audience has smartphones.

On top of that, the reality is that only about 6-7% of the population who own smartphones have actually installed (and know how to use) a QR-reader app.

And from those 6-7%, there is a strong bias towards young males who are tech-oriented.

So, in practice, although it looks 'hip' and 'must-have', the reality is that unless your target audience is using QR-reader apps, then right now they are not a necessity.

If you decide to use QR codes in your promotional material, here are a few tips and examples to help you create successful campaigns:

1. Make sure to have enough white-space around your QR code. If there isn't enough of a clean border between the code and the rest of your ad, then many older phones (yes, even smartphones) have serious difficulty deciphering the code.

2. Make sure to use managed QR codes where you can track the performance of your campaign and split-test yourself to success. Otherwise you're just shooting in the dark and probably wasting a lot of money in the process.

3. Don't limit yourself to promoting your own materials: once you've engaged users and/or enrolled them into your VIP program, you could follow the example JC Penny implemented over Christmas last year: when you buy a present for a loved one, you can record a short message. This message is then played when the recipient of the gift scans the barcode.

4. Add short informational videos to complex items in your store: again, the QR code redirects to a short video. This has e.g. been implemented very successfully in galleries, museums, triathlon stores and so on.

5. Think "social": you can do referral type competitions, where if someone buys a product at a friend's recommendation, the referrer gets a reward. This can make a strong impact on your social media presence.

6. You may have received a "Favorite Places on Google" card to put up in your shop-window: all this does is redirect a passer-by to a Google page about your business. You obviously want to make sure that the information the user finds at that site conveys the message you want to send out!

7. If you manufacture your own products, then you can provide more information, more of the backstory behind the product and of course an incentive to sign up for your SMS list through a QR code on your product.

8. Don't ever think about sending out a QR code in an email. Yes, people do this. And no, it's not really possible to take the camera phone off to scan the code in the email...

9. A similarly silly place is billboards by the roadside: unless you're willing to hop out of your car and walk up to the billboard, you're not going to be able to scan that code.

10. And no, you don't have reception in airplanes and subway stations, so putting your QR codes there doesn't make much sense either.

Summary

Over the last few pages we have taken a good look at why you may want to do mobile marketing, what you need to know to understand the technology, and how you might apply it in practice.

We had a look at the main technologies SMS, mobile website, mobile app, QR codes and coupons.

For most small businesses that sell mostly locally or at most regionally, we don't recommend mobile apps to begin with, and unless you have a rather young, male, tech-oriented target audience, you probably don't need to worry about QR codes just yet.

Instead, **we highly recommend you start building an SMS list**, most likely through the **use of a mobile website and coupons.**

Keep focusing on traditional advertising media like the newspaper, radio and TV ads, but start integrating them through everything you are doing online – **and SMS is a great tool for doing just that.**

Celebrate the fact that with mobile marketing it is now very easy and cheap to simply split-test yourself to success. And successful campaigns obviously mean higher turnover and profit, and often enough lower advertising costs.

When using SMS, you need to recognize that like many other technologies, it is just a tool.

And you still need to know how to use that tool.

As we've discussed above, consumers search very differently on their mobile device than on their PCs: their search terms and their intent are different, meaning the offers, the call-to-action, the coupons etc that work in traditional advertising, most likely are not optimal when it comes to the mobile medium.

The same goes for online advertising: if you are using pay-per-click (PPC) advertising, then you need to take into account the different mindset the user has when "on the go" — ads that work online, may well be a flop when used for mobile advertising campaigns.

The second big issue is that all of these technologies have to be integrated into an overall marketing strategy.

Especially SMS, which almost acts like the glue that holds all your marketing efforts together.

You constantly have to ask yourself what you are actually trying to accomplish and how can you use the mobile tools to achieve that goal.

At a more tactical level, you might be asking questions like:

- But how do I build my database?

- How do I design dynamic, compelling mobile campaigns?

- How do I integrate these tools into my overall marketing strategy?

If you would like to meet for a free consultation where we can help you with these questions, feel free to contact us at (706) 389-4796.

Trey

Trey Patrick

www.GeorgiaMobileMarketing.com

Trey@GeorgiaMobileMarketing.com

(706) 389-4796

www.ingramcontent.com/pod-product-compliance
Lightning Source LLC
Chambersburg PA
CBHW041106180526
45172CB00001B/137